I0158890

The Teeny Tiny Little Book with Everything You Need to Know About God

Jesh St. John

Published by OWL Publishing, 2026.

While every precaution has been taken in the preparation of this book, the publisher assumes no responsibility for errors or omissions, or for damages resulting from the use of the information contained herein.

THE TEENY TINY LITTLE BOOK WITH EVERYTHING YOU NEED TO KNOW ABOUT GOD

First edition. January 30, 2026.

Written by Jesh St. John.

Table of Contents

Why did you write this book?

Albert Einstein once said something like, "If you can't explain it to a six year old, then you don't truly understand it." then he famously went on to make many scientific discoveries that thoroughly confuse me. But then again, I never got to sit down face to face with him and give him a crack at explaining them to me. Maybe he could get through to me.

The point is, many things that seem extremely complicated on the surface, are actually fairly simple at their heart.

The entire gospel of Mark is only about 11,000 words long. That's about as long as a long-form ESPN magazine article—and it contains more truth than any person would ever be able to put into practice in this lifetime.

In fact, there are many single verses in the Bible that would take a lifetime to wrestle into understanding and put into practice. "But the fruit of the spirit is love, joy, peace, patience, kindness, goodness, faithfulness, gentleness, and self control..." (that's actually two verses, but who's counting?). 18 words... an eternity of wisdom.

So, if there's so much truth packed into so little space, why, you might be asking, is the Bible so gosh dern long? That's a great question, and I attempt an answer it later in this book.

There have been billions of words written about religion. You can get doctoral degrees about religion. People devote their entire careers to religion. The Jewish people used to train their children to memorize their entire Bible, which is more or less our old testament. The best students would go on to study scripture exclusively. Some would do so for the rest of their lives.

But when Jesus was selecting his posse, the people he would send out to light the fire of his church, he skipped all those educated sons-of-someones and went out to the lake to get some fishermen—literally. He got some everyday guys out of a boat.

C. S. Lewis, author of the Chronicles of Narnia and several other adult books about God and religion, was a professor at Oxford University in England. He was an adult when he first began attending church, and he had made a career of studying literature and ancient languages. He said that he thought he was going to be a big shot in his church because of all that knowledge.

Church congregations are a mixed family containing Christ-followers from all walks of life, and there was a simple farmer in that congregation. Lewis said that he realized very shortly that he wasn't fit to lick the soles of that man's boots.

Christianity is not about knowledge, and it's not about ability or experience. It's about the heart. Are you a person who loves what is right? Are you a person who wants to know what's true instead of what's popular? Are you a person who is willing to make sacrifices for other people? If so, then you're God's guy or gal!

I wanted to write this book because I think people sometimes make Christianity very complicated. It's not. The truth is actually very simple. Like many simple things, it can take a lifetime to put into perfect practice—you may also come to the end of this book and disagree with everything in it—but the information itself is actually very plain. I hope you find it that way in this book.

Who is God?

There had to be something at the beginning. That's simple logic. You don't get something from nothing. Scientists have traced the math all the way back to the moment the universe began. They call that event the big bang. That's where their trail goes cold. They can't see past that event.

Some scientists believe that the universe is in a cycle. It explodes, stretching outward like a balloon, and then eventually it slows down and then begins to come back inward. Eventually it compresses down into a tiny point of energy and mass, and then it explodes back out again. In that theory, the thing that was always here is the universe itself, sometimes big, sometimes small, but always there.

Some scientists believe we're in a giant computer simulation. But that just kicks the ball down the road a little further, because you have to ask, what computer? and who's running it?

There are all kinds of theories out there, some silly, some more serious, but they all eventually have to admit that something was there at the start.

Christianity teaches that the "thing" that was always there is actually a being. He's intelligent, powerful, fair, righteous, and loving. He created the universe on purpose. He created living creatures, including humans, and he cares about us deeply.

The Bible says that after creation, God walked with Adam and Eve in the garden. This means that his intention is to spend time with us. He wants to enjoy his creation with us. He wants to teach us, give us meaningful work to do, and help us to take ownership of his creation and make it a pleasant place to live.

When mankind went away from him, he took it upon himself to make a way so we could be united again. This took a great deal of patience, planning, humility, love, and suffering from God. We learn how to live best by following his example.

Can you prove God is real?

I'm going to get a little controversial here, because I personally do *not* believe you can prove God is real. Be careful, I didn't say that there's no evidence for God. I said you can't *prove* it. There's a whole branch of Christian study called apologetics which is devoted to the logical defense of Christian principles, and, often, to proving that God exists.

My thinking is that if God wanted us to have an airtight logical argument that proved he's real, then he would've included it in the Bible, which is his written word to us. I do not personally believe that God *wants* to prove he's real at this time. I believe this is because he wants to allow people to *choose* whether to follow him or not.

Think about the sun. It is outside every day producing light and heat. It is its own logical argument. The sun is real. It is evident to all people. Therefore, we all believe in the sun. There really is no choice in the matter.

God could easily show himself to all people in an undeniable display of power. In fact, the Bible says that one day he will do just that. But for now he chooses not to. If you're wondering why God would do that, take a look at the answer to the question about sin.

Having said that, there is evidence that points to God's existence all over the place. And it's not hidden evidence. The Bible says that he placed the knowledge of himself into the heart of every man. This is why people universally agree that there is such a thing as right and wrong. It's also why the human standard of morality is different from the one found in nature among animals.

There is also evidence in the natural world. The threshold for impossibility, or the statistical value where an event is classified as so improbable that, for all practical intents it is impossible, is cited at 1 in 10 raised to the power of 60. One non-Christian scientist estimated the probability that life would spontaneously evolve at 1 chance in 10 raised to the power of 340,000,000...

It's much more simple and logical to believe that an intelligent being made the universe with intention of purpose, beauty, and design.

This is why, despite the fact that intellectuals across the planet have rejected God, the debate continues. We all know deep down inside, despite the lack of logical *proof*, that there is a God. You have to squirm pretty hard to get rid of the feeling should you want to do so.

I do believe there is value in apologetics because, though I do not believe you can logically prove that God is real, I also do not believe you can prove that he is not real. Sometimes people are trapped in a place where they have believed some argument convincing them that God is not real. Apologetics can attack that false conviction, leveling the playing field back to a position where the heart of the person is allowed to speak clearly.

If you can't prove God is real, why do you believe in him?

I personally believe that God is real for the same reason I believe my wife is real—because he makes moves in my life. God set up a system whereby a person can tell very simply and easily that God is active in their lives.

Again, consider the sun. If some people experienced the sun as producing silvery light, and some people felt coldness radiating from the sun, and some people saw the sun as green, some blue, some pink, and some polk-a-dotted, then we would feel much less confident about what it truly is.

Instead, when my wife and I go outside on a sunny summer day, we both feel heat from the sun. We also both see bright, yellow light from the sun. The fact that we both experience the sun in the same way is strong evidence both in favor of the sun's existence and for what it does.

It is the same with God. When I read the Bible and read the apostle Paul's letters where he described what the Holy Spirit brought about in his life, I recognize things that he is doing, or has done, in my own life.

My grandfather was a strong Christian, and I saw him learn to live in a way that I now feel God teaching to me. My parents are Christian, and I see some of the same characteristics building in their lives that I see growing in my own.

God intersects the lives of believers in the same consistent fashion across time and place. This is strong evidence that he is real and consistent.

Now, having said that, there was a time when I was a young adult where God had not yet moved in my life because I had not yet accepted him. At that time, I had to take the initial step of believing in him based on much less personal evidence. I had to choose to love that impulse deep within me that argued in favor of right living, trace it to its source, which is God, and then respond. This is that step of *faith* that is so often talked about in Christian circles.

Believe it or not, my wife actually heard God tell her that he's real. She's not the first person to have God supernaturally intervene in her life, and she won't be the last. It is tempting to say that this is not fair—why should God supernaturally intervene with one person and not another?

I knew my wife before and after she began believing in God. She was the same person. Her heart was the same. She had a strong desire for Truth and a strong love of right living. In her case, God speaking to her was merely God stepping out of the natural course of everyday events to claim a heart that was already his. She could have ignored him.

The Bible says that after Jesus died, the religious leaders of the day posted Roman guards to stay in front of the tomb to make sure no one stole his body and claimed that he rose from the dead. They did it specifically because Jesus said he would raise from the dead, and they wanted to prove that he would not.

Angels came down from heaven to open up the tomb, and the Roman guards saw them. They ran back to tell the Jewish leaders.

Now, the Jewish leaders had heard Jesus's teachings. They knew the prophetic works of the ancient prophets that foretold Jesus's coming, his death, and his resurrection. They saw how Jesus lived. They had a front-row seat to his supernatural miracles, and now they had strong evidence that God himself was on his side because of the angelic intervention and the fact that he rose from the dead. They had every natural and supernatural opportunity to recognize and believe in the Son of God. So, what did they do?

They paid the soldiers to be lie. 'Nuff said.

Again, it's important to recognize the difference between evidence and proof. God provides plenty of evidence for his existence, but, for now, he's allowed everyone the free choice to snuff it out if they wish.

Do you actually think there's a Satan?

I do, and I actually think its really important. If you do not believe in Satan, then you have to believe that God made evil. As it is, I believe God *allowed* evil, but he did not make it. In fact, he *couldn't* have made it because evil is simply living against God's good plan and purpose. God can't stand against his own purpose.

No, Satan is the originator of evil. He was the one who was originally dissatisfied with God's intended purpose for his existence, and he was the one who originally went against God's design. He taught people to believe that God was holding something back and how to act in their own interest despite God's rules. He's still undermining our trust in God's ways to this day.

When you don't believe in Satan, you have to believe that all the impulses you feel that go against God's word in the Bible are your own natural self, created by God. Understanding that there is an enemy, and he is not you, allows you to take a stand against him. You are not quieting natural, God-given impulses when you work to quench sin or sinful impulses. You are working against an intelligent and strategic enemy who, because of hateful and jealous spite, wishes for your destruction.

If you are not a Christian this news is very bad, because how can you hope to conquer a spiritual enemy? If you are a Christian, it's wonderful news, because Satan was already defeated when Jesus died on the cross, and all that's left is to welcome the spirit of Christ in your life and allow him to drive the enemy out and repair anything that has been broken.

The work can be patient, plodding, and sometimes painful, but the rewards begin flowing immediately.

11

What is sin?

Sin is simply going against God's good design. It is a twisted version of something God made that was good.

Sinfulness can't exist without God's good creation. There can be no lie without the truth. There can be no stealing without provision. There can be no death without life. The reverse is not true. You can have truth without a lie. You can have provision without theft. You can have life without death. Sin is a parasite.

In the beginning, there was only one rule: Adam and Eve could not eat the fruit from one tree. They could eat from any of the other trees, and everything else was provided for, so there was no other sinful impulse.

I believe that the only reason God gave them the single rule to follow is because he wanted them to have a choice. He had created many thousands of animals that had no choice but to behave in certain ways according to their design. He wanted his special creation to *choose* to spend time with him.

This makes sense. It's not very romantic for a husband to give his wife flowers and a note that says, "Well, honey, I love you because I have to."

The original lie came from Satan. He got Adam and Eve to believe that God was holding something back from them. He tempted Eve to eat fruit from the one forbidden tree, and then Adam did the same. With that original sin, they put in place a separation from God. Just like when a child doesn't listen to his or her parents, he creates distance that usually separates the child from something that the parent means for good.

With separation from God, life became much more difficult. In the garden, everything they needed or wanted was there for the taking, but now they had to grow it, hunt it, build it.

With the work, there came much more reason for sinful behaviors. Man began to be angry, jealous, greedy, lustful, dishonest. Satan was still there as well, sowing seeds of every sinful feeling.

God's design was still good, but as the weight of sin increased, so did the distance between man and God. God was not satisfied with the way things were becoming because he saw the pain his creation was suffering, and he was saddened to be apart from them. So he began to work on a pathway for people to get back to him to regain their standing as his special creation and to regain their blessing.

Ultimately, this is the story of Jesus and his death on the cross, which we will discuss more later.

Sin does not happen in a vacuum. There are spiritual repercussions. When people sin they allow Satan to take a position of authority in their lives. When he takes that position, he works to keep the person in sin as long as he can.

This is one reason why sin is so destructive. It's not usually a one-and-done proposition. In the Bible, Paul describes this phenomenon as being a slave to sin. The only real way to completely get rid of sin and the enemy is to allow the Holy Spirit to help guide you through battle against it. More about the Holy Spirit later.

Another important characteristic of sin is that it is harmful. The Bible says that the wages of sin is death. This can play out in a number of ways, but I think the main point is that sin hurts something. This is why it's bad.

Lust isn't bad because God was thinking one day about how he could put a damper on our fun. It's bad because it damages a person's ability to be completely united with their spouse. There is no greater blessing on earth than to be completely united with one's spouse. So lust is not fun; it's destructive. Therefore, God is against lust. It truly is that simple.

Sometimes we have to trust him about why a sin is wrong. He may have reasons for saying something is wrong which we do not understand, but when we believe and understand that God is a good father who loves us, we can accept his rules and instructions happily.

We still have a choice whether to follow God's design or not. His way is the best, though it's not always the easiest. It does produce the best results for people who love goodness. If you don't love goodness, and instead you love, say, pleasure, then God's way is not going to be the fastest way to get what you truly want.

This is an important distinction, because I do believe that many people do not truly want what God is giving away.

Do you actually believe in eternal life?

I do, and here's why.

Remember from one of the first few questions that something had to exist forever whether it be the universe itself or a computer program or God. We believe that it is God that has always been and always will be.

If that's true, then I think there's two reasons we can be confident in eternal life other than the simple fact that God said it is so in the Bible.

One, if God truly loves us like the Bible says, and God has been around forever, then it would be rather ineffective for his own pleasure if death was the end of us. Think about it. God has been here forever, and you live, what? 80 years, then you're gone. To God that is literally a flash in the pan. Even the entire human history would be a flash in the pan. Creation would simply be like an exciting, but ultimately unsatisfying sparkler, flaring up for a minute, then disappearing. Each individual would be like a tiny spark from the sparkler, here for a moment, then gone. An all-powerful creator has no reason to not cause the creation that he loves to be around for as long as it pleases him, not a flash in the pan.

Second, the Bible is extremely clear that death is a consequence of sin. Sin was not God's design; it is a twisting of God's good work. If we ultimately die, then sin wins—God loses, and Satan wins.

First of all, this is unthinkable for an all-powerful creator. Second, this would invalidate Christ's sacrifice for us. He died on the cross so we could be free of sin. That has to mean that we're also free of death. If not, then there was really very little point to him dying.

Is there really a heaven?

There really is a heaven. There are answers to other questions above that address the plausibility of the existence of God, but if you believe that it's plausible for God to exist, it's really not that hard to believe in a heaven.

It's even less difficult to believe in heaven if you accept the fact that sin and death do not win out over God's goodness in the end. In the article on sin, we discussed that sin is a parasite. It cannot exist without God's good design. You can't have lies without truth, but you can have truth without lies. You can't have death without life, but you can have life without death. This is important because it tells us that if you take sin and death away, things go *back* to God's good design.

The Bible says that God will instate a new heaven and new earth which will be free from all sin and death. His people will live in that place with God, enjoying the majesty of his perfect and fulfilled creation forever.

What will heaven be like?

Heaven will be a place where right living will reign supreme. It'll be a place where sacrificial love will be everyone's daily pleasure to give. Generosity and contentment will be the standard. Humility will be everyone's coat to wear.

This all makes for a wonderful place to live. It will be a place that will need no law, not because the people will be lawless, but because every person who is there will love right living. They will all live in such a way that no official code will be necessary.

When the Bible talks about heaven, it uses a lot of imagery. It says things like that the streets are paved with gold. It also gives a very specific dimension for Heaven which turns out to be a cube. Some Christians believe that God intended for us to read those scriptures literally. I do not agree with them.

I believe that those images are meant to be symbolic. I believe the specific dimensions represent to us that Heaven will be the perfect size for all that it must contain. I believe that the images of golden streets are meant to convey to us that there will be no needs that are unmet. There will be such an abundance, in fact, that even precious gold will be very commonplace indeed.

There are more images, but outside of the imagery, the Bible is silent on what we can expect heaven to be like. However, there are some clues.

When Jesus prays the Lord's Prayer in the New Testament, he asks that God would make it "on earth as it is in Heaven." This cuts both ways. It tells us that the Holy Spirit will do work in us here that makes us more

Godly. It also tells us that when we see God doing things here, is is a window into what it's like in Heaven.

The Bible also tells us that God is the same yesterday and today and forever. This suggests that what was important to him at the moment of creation is still important to him today. In fact, it will always be important to him.

We know what God did when he had a blank canvas in front of him and could make whatever he pleased. This is the account of creation in Genesis. He made the earth, land, ocean, plants, animals, man, and woman. And the Bible tells us that all of those things were good, and so they still are.

I believe that when sin and death are stripped away it will allow all of creation to be the fullest and best expression of what God had in mind during creation. There will be varied plant and animal life. There will be natural beauty. There will be life systems and organization, chemistry, math, biology. It will be the ultimate fulfillment of God's original design, free for eternity from sin, death, and decay.

Mankind will revel in it, enjoying the perfect expressions of God's creativity forever.

Do you actually believe in hell?

I do, and here's why. God allows each person to freely choose whether to believe in him or not. Remember the story about the religious leaders paying the Roman guards to lie about Jesus's resurrection. They had every opportunity to accept the truth about Jesus, but they chose not to.

On the other hand, when Jesus was on the cross, two men were being crucified next to him. They were common criminals who had never met Jesus before. One of them poked fun at Jesus, the other defended him. This man had no real evidence that Jesus was anything special, yet he recognized the holiness in him. Jesus told the criminal that he would meet Jesus in paradise that day.

For people who truly crave the truth, it's not hidden. But plenty of people do not crave the truth. They crave pleasure or health or wealth or power or praise and recognition, but not righteousness, not holiness. They are not willing to give up their personal desires and aspirations in order to follow God.

This is important because it means that some people would *hate* to live in heaven. Heaven, as discussed earlier, is a place where righteousness will reign. It is a place where all of God's standards of selfless living will be the everyday standard of conduct, not because that standard is written into law and enforced, but because the only people in heaven will be people who love right living and God's leadership. It will be a joy and pleasure for them to live according to God's design in all facets of their existence.

The people who do not desire God's standards will be spared from having to live with them. Instead, they will be eternally separated from him. This may sound like fun for some people for a hot second until they realize that God made everything that is good. There is no joy without God. There is no peace without God. There is no love without God.

Without God, the sins and affects of sins will be allowed to run their rampant courses of destruction to their most bitter and disgusting ends. This will be a cup that no one will actually want to drink from. But it is the only alternative to life under God's leadership.

If God is good, why does he allow bad things to happen?

This is a three-part answer. First, God allows each person to choose whether to follow him or not because he doesn't want robots or instinctual animals for children. He wants a *loving* relationship with each of us, and that means we have to have the opportunity to choose him or not. Whenever we do not choose his way, it is harmful. Often, people choose to double down on incredibly harmful and destructive behaviors to the point where they seriously hurt themselves and others. Of course, God does not *like* this consequence.

Second, God allowed bad things to enter the world because he wanted to teach us about Love. True love is willing to endure hardship, even to death. Without the opportunity to endure hardship, we couldn't express our love as strongly as God intends.

When thinking about this point, it's important to remember that God didn't sit up in heaven above it all and let us sort out all the hardships of sacrificial love stuff down here on our own. He willingly showed us all how to love by coming down and being abused and killed for no other reason than to give it all back to us in the free gift of our redemption.

As a perfect and all-powerful being, there was no reason for him to humble himself, no reason for him to ever endure any pain or hardship. But he chose that path on purpose so he could show us how much he loves us. And ultimately, because sacrificial love is the path to all good things. He wanted us to know that, and he wanted to experience the Joy of loving himself.

Jesus said that he endured to the cross "for the joy set before him." The joy he was referring to is the joy of reaping the reward of sacrificial love. It's the greatest joy possible.

Without allowing bad things to exist, none of us would ever actually know the true extent of God's love for us. We would also not have opportunities to show others how much we truly love them.

Third, hardship and pain are not all-powerful. When people are not in relationship with God, under the lordship of Christ, and walking in his plans and purposes for their life, they are subject to whatever spiritual lordship they submit themselves to. This is never a safe place. God is always knocking, always trying to get in, but as long as the door's shut, the person is not under God's protection.

Christians, however, are under God's protection. We have to be careful here because I do not mean that anyone who *calls* themselves a Christian is under God's protection. Sadly, the church has many people in attendance who do not actually know and love God. But anyone who is truly walking with Christ and seeking his leadership in their lives will enjoy protection. The Bible says that God will set his guardian angels around us to protect us.

This sounds like a bold statement considering the fact that we see so much awfulness in the news. But the Bible is very clear on this point.

It's actually fairly easy to believe when you apply it to someone other than yourself. Ask yourself, was it ever possible that Jesus would get struck by lightning and die before he made it to the cross to die for the sins of mankind? Of course not. Could Peter have tripped and fallen down the stairs and died instead of taking his place as the first leader of the church? No. Was it possible that Billy Grahame could have gotten hit by a car as a teenager instead of walking out his calling to evangelize to millions of people? I think not.

The apostle Paul was bitten by a poisonous snake on one of his trips to spread the gospel. He simply shook the snake off into the fire. The people with him were amazed that he showed no ill-effects.

So, in the end, we're presented with a picture where bad things do happen, but not indiscriminately. God has the power and will to protect his own.

Beyond that, Christians are subject to various attacks from the enemy and other abuses. We are told in the Bible that the world will hate us. We are also told that Satan is strategically planning against us. This means that we will undergo various hardships throughout our lives even when we are under God's protection. The difference is, it won't be random, God will prepare us for the battles and be with us through them

As Christian, we are always on offense. The Christian's victories break down the strongholds of the enemy forever, sometimes to the benefit of the person him or herself, sometimes to the benefit of others.

In God's system, even death becomes merely a doorway to the fulfilled creation where God reigns and where everyone will know all the wonderful benefits of universal right living for eternity.

What's the deal with this Jesus guy?

When mankind sinned, a barrier came up between God and people. The relationship was broken, and there was no way for people to repair it. In fact, there was no real way for God to repair it either, because man had proved himself to be unclean. God is perfectly pure. He cannot be with impurity.

It was not as if God could just forgive this one time and then it would all go away. Once man started, man did not stop. It was constant, despite everything God did. He tried punishing. He tried giving rules and regulations. He even tried wiping the slate completely clean and starting fresh with someone he knew loved him (this was the flood and Noah on the ark). He tried blessing his people with everything they could want. He tried miraculous intervention. He tried isolating them. He tried everything. But man kept sinning, over and over and over and over again.

The chasm between God and man was infinitely wide. Since we insist on sinning, the only way we could ever repay him the debt we owed is if God could somehow figure out a way to accept our sin as payment for our debt.

We have nothing that he wants or needs. He made everything. If he needs more, he can make more. Additionally, our debt to God is infinite. Finite man cannot pay an infinite debt, so the only way for there to be an infinite payment would be if God himself found a way to pay it.

The way he did this was ingenious and unthinkably generous. He became a man so that he could pay the price for men. Then he lived a perfect life so that he never owed a debt. Then he allowed mankind to kill him undeservedly so that mankind owed him an infinite debt. Then he used that infinite debt to pay off, to his father God, the infinite debt owed to him from mankind.

And with every present and future sin, the Christ's death becomes less deserved, so man's debt to Jesus grows, and because of Jesus's infinite generosity, so does his payment to his father in our stead.

The generosity, love, and sacrifice inherent in this act, from both the father and the son are unfathomable. The fact that God gave his son—his *son,* his child, his boy!—up to the things he created, which he knew to be utterly unworthy, is unthinkably generous. The fact that the Son, being God, became a man at all is an unimaginable sacrifice, muchless that he allowed mankind to abuse and kill him. And the fact that he willingly hands the debt owed to him by us over to God as payment for our sins is love in action so powerful that we will never fully understand.

It's like if someone came into your house to steal a TV, you found him and said that he owed you a debt, and the only way that you would be able to consider the account as being cleared is if he came back and burned your whole house down. Then you'd be even. It's mind blowing.

In doing this, Jesus showed us the example of perfect sacrificial love that we get to enjoy living out with the people in our lives. He also won the privilege to claim anyone who accepts his free offer to pay their debt to God. There's no strings attached. We simply accept the offer. Then God comes into our lives and immediately begins to undo the yucky and twisted work that sin wrought in the place of right living.

Did Jesus really raise from the dead?

Yes.

I think the true barrier to believing that Jesus raised from the dead is really believing in God at all. If you can get over the hump of believing that there is a God, then I don't see it as a very big step at all to then believe that God has power over death. I covered why we can believe that God exists earlier in this book. If you cannot get there, then of course you wont be able to believe Jesus rose from the dead.

Having said that, if you believe in God and you believe the gospel that Jesus died for your sins, then you *have* to believe that Jesus also rose from the dead. If he did not, then he would still be dead, and death would have won. Sin would have conquered God himself. This, of course, cannot be. If it is so, then all is still lost, because we will all eventually still die, and thus, suffer the eternal penalty for our sins.

After we accept Jesus's free payment for our sins, our hope turns to the resurrection. This is how we will be able to actually enjoy the fullness of God's good design.

We *begin* to enjoy God's design on earth because God begins to change us immediately after we come to him. But because the earth itself is still broken, and people around us still sin constantly, we will spend this whole life working to restore and save. This is not God's ultimate plan for us. It is part of the toil of living in a broken world.

After Jesus died to pay the price for our sins, he rose from the dead, defeating death forever. Then he told the disciples that he was going to prepare a place for them. He then ascended into heaven. Because of

Jesus's example we can also hope for a new life and to join him in the wonderful place that he is actively preparing for us.

I keep hearing about this Holy Spirit thingy. What is that?

When Jesus defeated sin and death, paying the price for the sin of every man and woman who would accept his sacrifice, there was one problem: the world was still full of sin.

Sin was everywhere, and not only sin, but also Satan and his spiritual workers. As discussed before, when people sin, they allow Satan to take a position of authority in their lives. Entire historical societies were known to become consumed with sin. The early church had to fight many spiritual wars to overcome the spiritual forces which claimed those societies in order to fully overthrow their evil practices and beliefs.

Jesus never intended to fight a physical war like most people would have done. He also did not intend to go right to the top and work his way down. Jesus was after the hearts of individual, everyday people. He wanted the farmers and fishermen, the wives and mothers, the carpenters and doctors. This was true then and it's true now. He wants the average Joseph and Josephine, the commonplace Alex and Alexandra, the humdrum Jesh and Jeshuella.

But Jesus was a physical man. He could not be with each individual person himself. He could not personally wage spiritual warfare in all these different towns and cities at the same time. So he said he would send a "helper". By this, he meant the Holy Spirit.

The Holy Spirit is a spiritual being, one of the three members of God that make up the trinity (trinity explained later). The Holy Spirit lives with every believer. He guides, teaches, comforts, disciplines, and encourages, among other things.

He is the one who brings us to into battle with the sin in our lives, and he's the root of our hope that we can and will win battles against spiritual things. He's also the one who unites the greater church into the single cause of spreading the gospel into all the world and overthrowing the spiritual forces that are at work in any society that does rest on the foundation of God's truth.

He can be with us all at the same time because he's not constrained by physicality.

At its core, Christianity is personal. God meets everyone where they are. He designed you, so he knows you best. He knows your likes dislikes, desires, hopes, dreams, skills and abilities, problems, fears, etc. etc. And he navigates a relationship with each of his children with all those considerations in mind.

The Holy Spirit is the reason that it possible.

What is the trinity?

This is an area where I feel I could draw criticism from other church people because of my beliefs. The Trinity is supposed by many Christians to be a great mystery. God is three in one—God the father, Jesus the son, and the Holy Spirit. They are all fully God and yet, they are three. How can this be?

I have always simply thought of our U. S. government. There are three branches of government—the legislative, the executive, and the judicial. They are all the government, and the government is three branches.

Or a mommy and a daddy. They are both separate parents, but the two together are collectively the parents.

I'm sure many people will say I'm completely oversimplifying things. And maybe I am. But I have yet to reach the point in my everyday life where that "oversimplification" has affected me in any way whatsoever. So I think the illustration suffices for any practical intents and purposes.

Do you really think Jesus was born from a virgin?

I do. When God decided to free mankind from their sin, he had to take the burden to do so upon himself. No finite man could ever pay the price for every sin committed by every person. Only an infinite being could do that. But in order to pay man's price, he had to become man. He had to successfully navigate through life without sinning. This is what would make him the perfect sacrifice.

So he had to be both God and man.

If Mary, Jesus's mother had conceived Jesus through relations with a man, then Jesus would simply be a man. This would be fine except he could not pay the infinite price for the sins of all mankind.

Furthermore, Jesus himself said that he was more than a man. If this were not actually true, he would be at best delusional, and at worst, a liar. This would make him a sinner himself, and that would completely disqualify him from paying for all of mankind's sins.

If Jesus was not conceived through a woman, then he would simply be God taking the *form* of a man. This would also not suffice for his purposes because the payment for man's sins must come from a man.

So, we see that the virgin birth was actually one of the key strategic points in God's plan to win us back.

As to whether it *could* happen. Well, as I've said previously, the true hurdle here is believing in God. If you believe in God, it's not a stretch to think he could accomplish this, as incredible as it may be. If you do not believe in God, then of course it's not possible.

What is the Bible?

The Bible is a book written by human authors which conveys the word of God to mankind. It's text is inspired by God himself, and it is perfect. It is a trustworthy guide for living, and it conveys wisdom for people in every walk of life and every personal circumstance.

Many people refer to the book as "living." By this they mean that it applies to their lives in an uncanny way. They often find exactly what they need to know or learn from God in the text right as they need it.

While I completely and unreservedly agree with the sentiment—I myself have found this to be completely true in my own life—I do believe the term "living" could be slightly misleading to a new Christian.

I do not believe it is the *book* that is living or even really supernatural in any way. Rather, it is the Holy Spirit living inside each Christ follower who brings the text to life for them and points them to the scriptures they need when they need it. This is why unbelievers do not find the same life-giving properties when they read the Bible. In fact, the Bible says that even Satan knows the scripture. So, obviously, merely knowing what the Bible says will not set a person free.

How can you know that they got the right text into the Bible?

I'm not an expert in the historical process by which the books of the Bible were selected, but I do know that there are many religious texts that are not in the Bible. The books that were selected are collectively called the "canon", and it has been many years since the canon was changed in any way. So, it is valid to wonder, did they get it right?

Earlier in this book, when I was discussing why we can believe in a God when there is no logical proof, I talked about the fact that we trust in him because he moves in our lives, and because Christians all over the world give testimony (which is a churchy word which describes when someone tells about their own personal experiences with God) that he interacts with us all the same way. It is similar with scripture.

When we come to know the heart of God better and better over time, he molds the way we think, and we start to see wonderful threads of his truth weaving in and out of all of scripture. The text changes from a disjointed and tangled mess of unrelated tales to a beautiful tapestry.

It is not unusual for thematic strands to weave their way in and out of a text. But what makes the Bible unique is that the text was written over the course of thousands of years by numerous, very different people in numerous, very different walks of life. But still, the same themes carry through the entire book.

Furthermore, every true Christ follower will tell you that those same themes carry through the text into their own personal lives.

These are incredible statements to make about a book.

For example, there is a thread of sacrifice and freedom from slavery that weaves in and out of scripture. First, God tells mankind that a blood sacrifice is required to pay for sins. Later, He tells Abraham that he must sacrifice his son as an offering to God. God then stays his hand at the last moment and provides a substitute. Several hundred years later Moses is sent by God to Egypt to free the Israelites from slavery. The Egyptian king refuses to let the Hebrews go until God is forced to send an angel of death to take the first born of each household that is not protected by the blood of a sacrificed lamb. Some time after that, the prophets tell of a man who will be blameless, yet led to the slaughter. And hundreds of years after that, Jesus comes to fulfill all of it.

He is the blood sacrifice. He is God's own son sent as a substitute. He is the sacrificed lamb that stays God's angel of death. He is blameless before all people. His death frees all people from slavery.

Then, that same theme jumps off the pages of the book and into the lives of every true Christian the world over. Literally every true believer will testify that Jesus, through the work of the Holy Spirit, has freed them from the clutches of sinful or otherwise destructive behavior. Sometimes these are bad habits, sometimes crippling fears, sometimes physical ailments, sometimes addictions. The nuances of each specific instance are myriad, but they can be boiled down to that same theme which we read in scripture—the sacrifice God made for us frees us from slavery.

I only listed a select few of the places where this theme of sacrifice and freedom from slavery weaves in and out of the narrative of scripture. There are many more. And there are many other similar themes which do likewise. It would be unthinkable for such thematic development to occur by chance across thousands of years and many different authors. This is evidence that the text was chosen correctly.

As the years go on and I grow older with God, more and more of scripture resonates with me in that way.

What about those difficult passages in the Bible?

I hear this question a lot. People will point to a specific biblical story, like where God commanded the old-testament Hebrew people to kill everyone in a certain city, including women and children, and ask, how could God do it?

First off, I do not claim to understand all of scripture, but the more I see of God, the more I trust that there is good reason behind what he does. I trust that his movements are valid and just.

As difficult as it is for us to stomach, God created us. He does not need to justify any decisions to us including the decision to take any life whenever he chooses. In fact, he takes *all of our lives* at some point. That is literally true. We all die, and the Bible says that God is the one who's responsible for that.

We have to remember that this life is not everything. There is eternal life afterwards. God is fair and just to make sure that everyone is judged according to their own hearts. Everyone has and had a fair chance to accept God's truth.

Having said that, I do want to attempt to explain why I believe God gave those difficult instructions to the Israelites.

We have to remember that before Jesus, the Holy Spirit was not moving through the earth. But Satan and his spiritual beings *were* moving through the earth. Most cultures had adopted extremely evil practices.

God kept the Israelites relatively pure. They were to be his secret capsule—the way he would come in under the radar to launch his special mission through Jesus to save the whole world.

When Jesus came and conquered sin and death, the world changed forever. After his death up to today, when a person asks for God's forgiveness for a sin, God can simply give it because the debt is paid in full forever. That was not true before. Before, there had to be a payment.

But this did not just affect mankind, it also affected Satan. Remember what I said earlier in the book about the explanation of sin: sin places Satan in a position of authority in one's life.

Before Jesus, there was no real hope of getting out of that authority. This is why the Bible refers to it as being *enslaved* to sin.

In our modern world, the post-Jesus world we are used to, forgiveness is the keyword. We go on missions to bring the gospel of Christ's sacrifice and the forgiveness of God into dark and evil places. This frees people from the authority of Satan and drives the enemy away. The gospel does the work for us.

But back in ancient times, Satan's authority was much more difficult to unseat. In fact, before Jesus, the only way to rid a place of evil was the death penalty. God's people used sacrifices to pay that penalty, but pagan peoples did not. The difficult truth is that the wages of sin is death.

Importantly, that did not change when Jesus died on the cross. That fact is still true today. The wages for sin is still death. The only difference is that we have God's own death to accept as payment in place of our own. God chose to do this for us by his own free will.

I believe that God is fair in all things. The Bible says that in our earthly life we only understand in part, but in heaven we will understand in full. In heaven, we will learn how God was fair and just in all things.

The Bible says that this earthly life is like a vapor. It is the eternal life which we should have our hearts set on. Many people will lose their earthly lives and gain eternal life. It's a good trade.

If God's truth is so simple, why is the Bible so gosh dern long?

God's truth is simple, but the Bible was written by God to apply to every circumstance that man or woman may encounter. It's meant to cover every walk of life, every sin, every spiritual question, and every good and righteous thought or deed. It must be able to encounter literally anyone, no matter where they are in their lives and bring them hope and truth.

Obviously, with the vast variety of people and the differences in their lives, it has to be a large book.

What I have found is that not only did God create a book that functions as described above, but he did it with flair. Other than his creation, the Bible is truly the creator's greatest work of art.

I'm doing just fine. Why do I need God?

There's a few reasons. The first is that God made everything that is good. If you are enjoying financial freedom, God is the one who first conceived of the idea that people should have everything they need and want at their fingertips. That's why he put Adam and Eve in the Garden of Eden.

If you are enjoying a wonderful relationship with your spouse, God was the one who created romantic love. He made Adam and Eve for each other. In fact, the only thing that was not good in the original creation was that man was alone. Creating Eve and bringing them together perfected God's design.

If you are enjoying a fulfilling career, it was God's idea that every person should have purpose. The Bible says that, "I know the plans I have for you, plans to prosper you..." God created each person unique and has plans for them that uniquely utilizes their characteristics.

Those are some of the many good things that God has designed for his people, and if you are experiencing them, then don't you want it more and better?

The more I walk with God, the more I find that he wants to wake up *all* of me. It takes time, but God wants to use every bit of the man he designed. He works in me toward that end daily. And as I cooperate with him and grow and develop, I get to enjoy living in that design which fits like a glove.

God wants your whole existence to be full of wonderful blessing. His promise is that even if we do not experience all God's blessings on earth, we will in heaven for eternity.

The second reason is that all men die. You may be doing great now, but what about in fifty years? You will grow old. Your body will lose its vitality. What then?

I've heard many people say that when they finally pass on, it will be for the better because they will have lived a full life. This is unsatisfying. You may feel that way when you're 88 years old and can barely walk, but no 25 year old feels that way.

It doesn't work because it's circular logic. "I'm okay with my body breaking down completely because it's already broken down a lot, and I'm okay with my body breaking down because eventually it will break down completely." That doesn't make sense.

God's promise for his people is eternal Life. This means more than just living forever. It also means living in God's perfect and wonderful design forever. It means a restored body that does not break down. Our eighty-something years might seem like a lot now, but compared to eternity, it's just an instant.

The third reason is that there are certainly ways that you are living that are not according to God's design. This is true for everyone to a greater or lesser extent. But life with God means that those things become less and less over time.

When sins are in your life, they are destructive. You may not see it or feel it, but it is happening. You may go your whole life in blissful ignorance of the destructiveness of your sins, or you may someday discover it with sad consequences. But either way, it's happening.

Lastly, God made you and loves you. He designed you. He knows you better than any person could ever know you. There is nothing more fulfilling than living in harmony with your creator. It's truly like discovering your long-lost father and finding that he's always loved you, always cared for you, always wanted to be with you, and knows ways to build you up and provide for you that you couldn't have even guessed yourself.

So even if you're doing pretty swell, there's more and better waiting.

I'm a good person. Isn't that enough?

Being a good person is to being a Christian what being strong is to being a Marine.

You can't walk into a local gym, go to the free weights, find the biggest, strongest guy there, and assume he's a soldier. That would be silly.

Marines are not free to use their strength however, wherever, and whenever they please. They are not even free to develop it however they please. They must follow a strict training regime dictated to them from far over their heads. That training regime is created with plans and purposes in mind.

Marines will then use their strength and training in a specific place and time to accomplish a specific task as determined by military leadership. On the battlefield they may even be in situations where they have to pass by opportunities to use their strength in ways that could help their comrades in order to fulfill their specific mission. In short, a Marine's strength is not their own. It is an asset of the American government

The same is true of Christianity. Christ followers do not pursue goodness in a general sense, lashing out with wholesome behavior at any and every opportunity that presents itself; they hone their goodness according to God's specific mission for them, their calling, and cut with precision, like a surgeon, to address specific tumors in their environment.

Christ followers have specific callings and purposes. God speaks to them. He leads them to act or not act as his perfect goodness and wisdom wills. It is *his* responsibility, not ours, to ensure that fairness and justice is served throughout his whole creation, and he will accomplish this task. Sometimes it is by asking us to act, sometimes not. A Christian's goodness is not his or her own. It is an asset of God.

Furthermore, a person who is merely good does not share in the wonderful joy and freedom which comes from knowing God personally as a father. The creator of the universe wants to know you. He wants to teach you how he designed life to be lived. Being a good person is a grey substitute for that personal intimacy.

What will change if I become a Christian?

When you become a Christian, you accept Christ's payment for anything that you may have done that went against God's perfect and loving design. Immediately, the same instant that you give yourself over to God, the Holy Spirit begins working in your life.

So, what does he do?

Well, before you were a Christian, you did many things that were against God's design. Since everything God designed is good and healthy for us, going against that design is destructive. These things are collectively called sins. But not only are there harmful consequences that you may or may not be aware of, sin also puts Satan in a position of power in your life.

It is also possible that you may have inherited some sins from your parents. Think of the third-generation alcoholic. It is not coincidental that sometimes bad behaviors move down through families. Sometimes there are physical reasons, sometimes genetic, and sometimes spiritual, but no matter how they get there, they are destructive, and God wants to get them out of your life.

The Holy Spirit wants to free you from any and all destructive consequences of behaviors. He doesn't care where they're from or who started it, he wants to bring you out and place you in a healthier and more prosperous place.

Depending on your history or the heritage you received from your parents, you may have more or less baggage to work through to get to that place. It may be a lifelong journey. It may take multiple generations before your descendants fully work out of all the yuck, but God will do it. The Bible says that God does not fail to complete any good work that he has begun in us.

God will also begin to bring you into good and purposeful work for his glory and the benefit of people around you. He will tailor this work to how he designed you and to what your strengths and weaknesses are. As you walk further and further out of sin, you will walk further and further into God's perfect plan for your life.

I love the story of the man who was crucified with Jesus. He was a common criminal, but he defended Jesus to another common criminal who was also being crucified. That man had only minutes or hours to live, but Jesus immediately went to work redeeming him—Jesus comforted him and gave him hope by telling him that he would be with Jesus in paradise that very day.

God also displayed his wonderful ability to bring purpose to every person's life by using that man's very short time left on earth to provide a testimony and witness to millions of future people of the fact that it's never too late to turn away from sin and come to Christ. It all happened in the last minutes of that man's life.

Most of us have more time than that. My experience is that the changes the Holy Spirit makes seem much smaller and less significant than we expect. But as time goes on and the days turn into months, and the months turn into years, all those subtle and seemingly insignificant baby-steps cause a massive divergence from your previous course.

It's just like if you draw two lines, one angling away from the other by only 1 degree. At first, they are incredibly close to each other, and the divergence seems insignificant, but as you follow those lines out away from their intersection, the further you get away, the more distance there is between the two lines. Soon enough, there is a universe of difference between the two courses.

How do I know if I'm a Christian?

The Bible says that we can tell if people are Christians by their fruit. By this, he means that the *fruit of the spirit* will be evident in the life of a Christian. The fruit of the spirit is love, joy, peace, patience, kindness, goodness, faithfulness, gentleness, and self-control. If you are a Christian you will see the fruit of the spirit developing in your life. These changes can be slow, but certainly as months turn into years you will see growth.

The testimony of good spiritual fruit is universal to all true Christ followers since the time of Christ over two thousand years ago.

Here is a (incomplete) list of things God does for his followers: He'll identify sin. He'll bring your conscience to life. He will attack any spiritual forces that have set up shop to oppose your healthy growth and movement. He will begin to cultivate good qualities of character in you. He will plant the seeds for tasks that he will have you do in the future. He will challenge you to love others sacrificially, and not just for your own benefit. He will give you work to do that will bring his light and truth into the world around you. He will begin to mold and shape you to become more like his original, perfect, and unique design. He will work in the physical world to create more comfort, better living, and fuller health. He will work to break bad habits which steal health or money or comfort from you. He'll challenge your preconceived notions, your secular education, and any incorrect beliefs. He'll begin to replace these with truth from the Bible. He'll illuminate scripture for you, showing you how to read and understand the narrative of his purpose through history, his plan for the future of mankind, and your place in it. He'll build in you a hope for eternal life. He'll unveil for you the beauty of his creation. He'll teach you about how he designed life to be lived, both in a general sense as it applies to mankind, and a specific sense, as it applies to you and your family. Most importantly, he will show you how much he loves and cares for you, not in a general sense, but in a specific sense, as his own child who he knows intimately.

But with all of these things, you should see and feel an active *outside* hand participating in the work to make you whole. It *is not* the same thing as self-improvement. It does not come from more or better effort. If you do not see these things happening in your life, and you do not feel an outside, personal force acting in your life, then you have very serious cause to wonder if you are truly a Christ follower.

When I become a Christian do I have to act weird or give up the things I love?

Becoming a Christian is, in many ways, not so different from, say, finding a new amazing burger place. I remember the first time I ate a Five Guys burger. Someone who had eaten there told me about it. When I went, it was incredible. Since I enjoyed it so much, I told my friends about it. I went with some of those friends to eat it again. Some of them loved it; some not so much. I enjoyed it so much that sometimes I would drive out of my way to have a burger for lunch—it changed some of my habits.

If you're not a fan of Five Guys, hopefully you still get my point. When people turn to God and allow him a place of leadership in their lives, he changes them for the better. When they experience his goodness, they want to share it. This is only natural. When they experience his truth, they want to spread it around. Again, this is only natural.

There's no rule that says you *have to* talk about God to X number of friends within the first year. Some churches really push this point, and I disagree with them. I believe the Bible describes a model where the blessings of God *overflow*. If you are in relationship with God and it doesn't happen to boil over in that way, great. That's not an issue. Maybe it will later. Maybe God has other work for you to do.

But what will happen for certain is that over the course of time you will feel yourself changing. God will teach you about his creation. It's like watching a great documentary about a sport you love. You learn about the history, the design of the game, and you grow to love it more. You think about it a little differently. If you play the sport, you may even play it differently.

When you learn more about life the way the designer designed it, you live that life differently. You just do. It's only natural. It would be much more strange if you lived it the same.

You will have friends with whom you used to see eye-to-eye that you will now disagree with about some things. This is only natural because they are not listening to the designer of the universe as he teaches about his design.

God will also begin to bring out his special, unique design in you personally. He will have work for you to do that will take a person of your skills and ability. He'll show you how he created you to enjoy certain things, and he will ask you to leave some other things behind. This is all because he knows you very well, and he has intentions for your development and growth.

This is no different from a father or mother who helps to advise their children on what college courses to pursue. They do it out of love because they know their children very well.

As all of this happens over the course of years, or decades even. Your tastes will change. You will become a very different person in a lot of ways. But it will all be good. None of it will be bad, no, not a single thing. He is that careful and that thorough.

How do I hear God?

It's God's responsibility to lead you more than it's your responsibility to hear God. Having said that, it *is* your responsibility to listen and then to obey when he does speak.

There's a story in the Bible where a boy named Samuel is working in the temple of God. He lives, works, and sleeps there, and there's a priest who lives, works, and sleeps there also. One night, Samuel hears a voice calling his name, "Samuel, Samuel."

He runs into the other room where the priest is sleeping and asks him what he wants. The priest tells him that he did not call him, so Samuel goes back to sleep.

Then he hears the voice saying his name again, "Samuel, Samuel." He runs into the other room and asks the priest what he needs. The priest tells him that he did not call him, so Samuel goes back to sleep.

Samuel hears his name one last time, "Samuel. Samuel." He runs in to see the priest, and this time, the priest realizes that it must be God who is speaking to Samuel, and he tells him, "Next time, you respond, 'Speak Lord, your servant is listening.'"

I love this story because I think it illustrates an essential characteristic of a Christ follower: someone who listens to God. When Samuel was thinking merely in human terms, he ran three times to his caretaker to ask what he needed from him. But God was not moving toward Samuel from that direction. The solution: a simple change of posture. Samuel turned his ear toward God.

When you believe in God in faith and turn your ear toward him for his leadership with intention, you find him speaking often. He is not speaking incessantly, but he does speak often.

It's rare that God speaks audibly. I do believe that God does sometimes speak in dreams and visions. I do also believe that sometimes God will use another Christian to bring his word to you. We also have the support of God's word in the Bible, and we can often rely on the wisdom of church leaders. But I believe that God also often leads us in the form of spiritual tugs and nudges.

It's difficult to describe exactly what this feels like, but I'll attempt it. For me, I would describe it as sort of an ethereal stamp of authenticity that is attached to a thought or emotion. Just an almost subconscious notion that you can't quite shake that, "Oh, yeah that's true."

It's a gentle stamp, easy to ignore, but what happens is that you begin to follow those tugs and nudges and they compound one upon another, until at some point in the future you look *back* and you see, "oh my, I've come pretty far." And then you compare the fruit of your progress with scripture, and sure enough, it lines up with what the Bible said the Holy Spirit will bring.

This confirms for you what you had suspected and you grow better at recognizing those subtle tugs and nudges. It also encourages you to keep persevering in the same direction.

I've spoken to God before, but I've never heard him speaking back to me. What's Wrong?

It could be that God is speaking some other way, like through a pastor or friend. It could be that God has nothing to say right now, because you're moving along where you should be, and he's not making any course correction.

But it could also be something else. The Bible says, "Seek and you shall find. Knock and the door shall be opened to you." By this, it means seek *God* and you shall find *God*.

God is not a comfort vending machine. He is not a financial freedom vending machine. He is not a physical health distributor. He is not here to simply serve your needs and desires.

Having said that, he does do all those things for his children, but that's not how we approach him. We shouldn't think of him simply in those terms.

This may sound confusing, so think about a child's relationship with his or her parents. The parents provide food and shelter, clothes, education, love, support, etc. But if the child suddenly one day said, "From now on, all I want from you is food and a house." That would not go over well. Or even if he said, "You're job is to love me, so start loving me more."

If the child isolates one or more of the services that the parents provide and attempts to remove it from the context of the relationship, that is idolatry. It's incredibly hurtful for the parents who selflessly love their child.

God is the same way. He loves us unconditionally. He wants a *relationship*. The Bible describes our relationship with God over and over again in terms of the relationship between a father and his children. We must approach God in that light. We must approach him humbly, like a child. We must approach him with respect, with obedience, with love, with admiration, with tenderness, and with an attitude intent on learning, not directing.

I have found that when people are struggling to hear God it's often because they have some underlying agenda. They may not even be aware of the fact, but it's there.

When you attempt to approach God, approach him as a son or daughter would approach a good father. Approach him with deference and trust. He won't fail to lead.

How do I become a Christian?

The Bible says if you believe in your heart and confess with your mouth that Jesus is Lord, then you will be saved. It can be done at any time and any place. Now, in fact, may be a great time to start. It really is that simple.

It's also really that hard.

Admitting to yourself, in your heart, the core of your being no less, that there is a Lord of your life and it's not you is no light matter. It means that you admit and accept that there is an intelligent being who has plans and purposes for your life and who is in charge.

But the wonderful thing is that you are no longer responsible for making your own way through the world. God loves you, and the plans and purposes he has for you are wonderful and personal. He takes responsibility to lead and guide expertly, to provide and protect powerfully, and to comfort and affirm lovingly.

So after you make that decision, what do you do? Begin listening. This is a simple change of posture. You now pay attention to the Holy Spirit instead of simply reading and reacting to your physical environment.

It would be very wise and helpful to begin reading the Bible. This is especially true if the Bible was not ever taught to you. It will be a shortcut to understanding many of the things God will teach you. It will also give God some material to begin working with.

Remember, it is God's responsibility to lead. It is his responsibility to teach. It is truly very similar to a father and child relationship. The father has the responsibility to mold the son or daughter. Children should not have to pull their own education and direction out of their parents.

Begin cutting away at known sinful behaviors. It is God's responsibility to break them away for good, but your goodwill participation is also needed.

Find a good solid church and begin attending. Having a group of other believers around you to help guide and pray for you will be one of the chief ways that God brings his goodness to fruit in your life.

To clarify, the only thing you *need* to do to be saved is to believe in your heart and confess with your mouth that Jesus is lord. All the rest of it is just wise action. It will be beneficial to you as a budding Christian. It is not necessary for your salvation. If you don't do one or all of the things, it does not mean you're not a Christian. However, these are almost certainly things that God, as your loving Father, will want to see you do so that he can bring peace, joy, purpose, and right living into your life powerfully, efficiently, and permanently.

About the Author

Jesh St. John is a husband and a father. He married the love of his life, his high-school sweetheart, in 2011 and set about the urgent business of raising a family. They are blessed with five strapping boys and one girl. Well, four strapping boys, one girl, and a squishy baby.

The St. Johns live in Northwest Ohio, just south of Lake Erie, where they run a small business, raise animals, and feed the community sports teams.

Read more at www.JeshStJohn.com.

www.ingramcontent.com/pod-product-compliance
Lightning Source LLC
Chambersburg PA
CBHW060536030426
42337CB00021B/4288